THE PRO
OF RES

An anthology of poems
from Ragged Raven Press

2002

Ragged Raven Press

Snitterfield, Warwickshire

THE PROMISE OF REST

First published in England, 2002 by Ragged Raven Press
1 Lodge Farm, Snitterfield,
Warwickshire CV37 0LR
e-mail: Raggedravenpress@aol.com

website: www.raggedraven.co.uk

The promise of rest
ISBN 0 952080796

Set in Arial.

Printed by Antony Rowe, Bumper's Farm, Chippenham, Wiltshire
SN14 6LH

THE PROMISE OF REST

The fourth anthology of poems
from Ragged Raven Press

2002

CONTENTS

FOREWORD

Welcome to our fourth anthology of contemporary poetry, *The promise of rest*, which is a result of submissions that have come in to us over the year and a selection of entries to our annual competition. Work by the competition winner, Mike Parker, and the runners-up, Margaret Eddershaw and Jocelyn Simms, is featured, plus poems from John Robinson, whose book *the cook's wedding* we published in October 2001. Other contributors include Australian poets Kelly Pilgrim and Bron Bateman. Their joint collection is Ragged Raven's next book, which will be published in June 2002.

Some poets in *The promise of rest* have had their work included in previous Ragged Raven anthologies. Others appear here for the first time. We very much hope you will find plenty to enjoy.

Our leaning is towards more experimental and expansionist poetry rather than versifying trapped by traditional ideas of form. Basically, we believe a poem is, or should be, an independent, complete verbal event, which is paraphrasing a description offered by Canadian poet Margaret Avison and quoted in a recent edition of *Poetry News*.

If you would like to know more about Ragged Raven Press, please contact us or visit our website: www.raggedraven.co.uk Feedback on any of our books is always welcome. We have no external source of funding and rely on sales to survive.

Janet Murch, Bob Mee

Cover drawing by Lizzie Mee.

Poetry from Ragged Raven Press:

Old songs getting younger (anthology) £6 ISBN 0 9520807 5 3

Smile the weird joy (anthology) £6 ISBN 0 9520807 6 1

Red Hot Fiesta (anthology) £6 ISBN 0 9520807 7 X

the cook's wedding by John Robinson £6.99 ISBN 0 9520807 8 8

MIKE PARKER

Elizabethan gentlemen on The Thames 1599

A wallet of night, a thin skiff,
both, wait on the water; your lyre
lays in the gunwale and the cliff
of darkness in this past
holds its hung, wave-shape fast
against your hurried rower's hire...

(The day's drunk details kept the sky
away, and meats in many reds
were either vital or denied:
the dead eaten, the caught
bear and mastiff fought
until the living and dying, bled.)

...When lightning sears a caesar scar
along the river's live tissue,
twelve thousand lanterns die, their stars
lost in the greater flash.
They are water and ash,
the gentlemen, glowing wishes.

The river knows they're dead people
as they live, so they feast and song
as they tipple under steeples;
yet Awe is their moral,
and the chopped water calls
to come, to be gone, to float along.

Brine and Fresh, mix their salt and clear
tingle, at the tide's pushing point;
the sky's hands on your shoulders steer
you to bank, land and Inn,
to beer and table; shin
beef's juices, red-wet in the joint,

painted in whorls like a cosmos,
printed by a god's finger, ringed
with weep loops, a cut trunk across,
next to pickles and conserves.
Every song preserves
them in the rhythm of a hymn.
Sing today's meaning, gentlemen,
on water cheat oblivion.

MIKE PARKER

Young portfolios

I

The youthful functioning of any anatomical system, either sexual glands, digestive apparatus, or muscles, is very dangerous for old men.   *Alexis Carrel*

buck strut   cock crest   indecent
                  priapic pensioners
lumbered with lust's risk
passion points them out
   they can't   reach   the symbolic

...the Heart asks and asks...

the Liver filter
fat tongue tasting Iron
demands of blood
cleaning the poisons
fighting filth
     in a ceaseless system

where's peace   rest and acceptance?

frantic
the same rages
plague each age
ancient angers and new bile
corrugated
     in a
         slippery   splenetic jackcracker

...to never forgive to never have forgiven?...

those Kidneys
     they

11

muslin sift corruption
in their round alembics
  rivers and rain   urine
pure policy become
                regime
                doctrine
                when
the forgetful brain   should've forgotten blame

    got
wet gut
hard arm
full lungs
chipper intestines

when...
   ...isn't sanity   madness worn out?...

II

Abnormally vigorous organs in a senile organism are almost as
harmful as senile organs in a young organism.   *Alexis Carrel*

portfolios between
   their knees
beautiful   open
       young men

after an art of experiment
                and abstraction

first free feelings
and the conceptual

  visualised
   from
       their truthful studios

who would warp them with wisdom?

they'll wash the old patron's
back in the bath
without his circumspection

dry his hair
into his chosen convention

                        then
like coral in glass
the stem inside accretions
benthos in ice
a pip in flesh

                the young man
        I was
                is suspended
so   open   open
        the portfolios
        of those other
                young men

                them
                them

MIKE PARKER

Aunt's Agony

Like a political memory - a detainee - a forgotten warrior disgraced
Aunt came back to us   blinking shaking
35 years of barrack tea in The Chapel's shadow and the Ward's lights

the drugs have changed since she tore Grandma's arm
with fingers like robot lazers she atoned through delirium
locked wards underground screaming horrors
loud trays and trolleys bashed by beaters for grouse
Simba hunters - scared rousers in pampas foliage and frightened
                                                            grasses

she paid the usury sane their catastrophic rate

when she was seventeen a slim sailor damped the wick
of her little glass lamp heart   her frailty condemned her
could a tree surround a core rot with tough new rings?
the barrel burst

the madness of an Aunt adds a living gene to a family's disposition
amino-anima Fear Implicated We are together and alone
with our kin's crazy genome which like a quake might strike
any one of us we search the days for signs while we deny signs

huge in her helplessness Aunt dominated us from her torture
gibbering on the spot   we waited fearing the medication in our slobber

between our visits clever and mad Jacobs allowed her dreams
lending their ladders to her pain twice she escaped
despite her slow hips magnetised legs and rot yellow nails
looking like a secret synthetic breakthrough chemical weapons

her right arm shook a bandleader's beat unknown to music
her broken probe lurched home from the alien mental
she frightened everyone as if we wished our minds
were drawings in 3-D like cupboard boxes   containers
holding a jumble of normal life in more or less disorder
a wedding drawer of Being a marginal scruff shelf

resumed
  she wore frocks in half-way houses and denied cancer
skinnier citizens played the untuned piano the hallway smelled of fish
her sisters visited her nieces sent trinkets in the endless
conflict between residents she tore another arm still scary strong

madness whittles its victims to thin furniture
or bloats them like sentimental overtures
we the family moderates looked to our figures
keeping our lives small and shorebound   the sea
its vast erotic back of water is for the sensual sailors.

JOCELYN SIMMS

Mischanter

Rain stiffens hedgerows
packed with hips and brambles
hung with purple vetch.

This larder is full. Jar on jar
preserved for leaner days.

The baby would be born now
as the leaves turn from green
to gold to red.

My finger slides from the pinked
edge of greaseproof to the lop-sided
label. *Blackberries 1975*.

Fold away the muslin cloth. Set
the long-handled spoon in its shiny
pan. The ground will harden. And birds
will feast.

JOCELYN SIMMS

Under My Skin

April 1962 and something's got
to give at the walled-in
hacienda on St. Helena Drive
a smell of dog crap stings the air

edgy as a ballerina
she stares at pool-blue water
grimy cracks fissuring
between her crimson toes
she does not bathe

poised at the cocktail hour
her mirror shows a candyfloss
creation - transparency of net
a bauble twirling

and swirling her juice
sweet as barley sugar
for a sugar sphinx

at two in the morning
close to jumping out of her skin
she sinks seconal/nembutal/
chloral hydrate to cool

the pillow the locked
and shuttered room
drapes nailed down
silencing the dark

her gown slips from the chair
spills its froth with a crackle
lying awkward stiff
waiting for the red-eyed dawn

JOCELYN SIMMS

Pond Life

we close until our shadows
bow, one to the other,
entangle on a makeshift raft:
the pearls I wear
dissolve like rain

nightshade advances
beneath the deadly pear,
gilded fruit drips
through our fingertips,
smudges
this frozen lawn

from copper deeps
your resilient toe draws
a glitter-chain, trawls
silver leaves, spinning light,
salvaging this fretwork
of floating weeds

MARGARET EDDERSHAW

All at sea

Confusion masked by the smile
he waits for me to tell him who I am
proudly exhibits for the n'th time
his room crowded with a lost past

I used to build boats, you know
This mantra throws a line ashore
to curtail his anchorless drifting
near unremembered coasts

He doesn't know it
but he is mostly the father I knew
sociable, humorous
with flashes of inexplicable anger

Eyes bright with innocence
thin skin glowing over cheeks
small yet strong, so familiar hands
belie the bewilderment in his head

Cranial caulking has leaked
so again he asks my name
politely as though at the captain's table
He surveys the photos on the mantelpiece

like a marooned sailor scanning the horizon
for the rescue boat
I frame every sentence with *Dad*
but that word's meaning is a castaway, too

He shakes his healthy shock of hair
like a dog trying to reorganise its ears
He can find no clues in my face
so examines his shoes

from which he has again cut the laces
Bought these in Portsmouth during the war
Another mantra
He fingers his buttonless cardigan

having taken against buttons, too
To tell you the truth, he laughs
as though beginning a joke
I have no idea where I am

My hesitation at the existential question
allows him to forget he ever wondered
and he's all at sea again
too far out to see me wave

MARGARET EDDERSHAW

Museum whispers

Through fissures in time
I caught her icy breath
knew her in an instant
her shame as she was dragged from gaol
a man's jacket over the flannel petticoat
to be cargoed on her first ever boat
In her sighs chains dragged on salty decks
weird howls shook the rigging

planks groaned fit to split
women shrieked like rats in a pail
She took my hand and I felt her calluses
As we creaked upstairs she whispered
of the terrible heat as they landed
A pasty English soldier in arrogant red
hammered shackles from her seeping ankles
vast land and seas were now the chains

In semi-darkness I gazed at keepsakes
a child's shoe, faded locks of hair
From sun up to sun down my guide intoned
work, beatings, fighting for food
just like the great hunger she laughed
drifting softly towards the next room
Her finger traced the name of Mary Keogh
gaoled for ten years for stealing a hat

I had to buy bread she breathed in my ear
Eighty hammocks crowded the third floor
their faded fabric wefted with tears
warped with repeating nightmares
agonies shared by strong women
become children in the stinking dark
Sunlight darted now through upper windows
Mary had married a ticket-of-leave man

turned vile punishment into possibility
yet she felt my sorrow at her dispossession
Her smile shivered down my arms
*Roots are **inside*** she said vanishing into
the stark light of a December afternoon
and on the still air I heard the jaunting
of fiddle, flute and drum

STEPHEN STEINHAUS

Got Nuthin'
In front of Aardvark Books, 16th and Mission, San Francisco

My son is strapped to my back
as I browse the music section in the back aisle at Aardvark
the store itself is littered with the upscale refuse of the city
among whose numbers...I must now count myself.

It's a new city and we hate it
collectively, that is,
though my boy is asleep.
As he snores, I'm scanning down the shelves.

I can feel his weight pushing down at the base of my neck
as I strain to thumb through the shelf for what I need.
I stand up awkwardly as the blood rushes to my head.

I stagger back.

My son stirs momentarily then settles again
his cheek is hot, damp against the skin of my neck
rising over the collar of my T-shirt.

Looking at that shelf, my eyes glaze for a second.

It stinks like cats and sweat in this place
and the dog in the front has a festering sore on its leg

a sore   he won't   stop   licking

so, I push my way through the dross and out into the street.
the sun and stench of the street hit me in the head
as the J-train rumbles past,
kicking up debris in its wake.

A homeless guy in a torn yellow jacket
and rotting baseball cap
nods at me

I am not in the mood so I ignore him and step to the right

Spare any change, big man? he says
in a voice of vomit and vodka
I don't even look at him

Got nothin', man, I say
but his hand stops me.

He doesn't touch me or anything
but, out of the corner of my eye
I do see him point over my shoulder

Naw, dude...don't say that...
he says, grinning, still pointing at my son's half-buried face
you got him...

STEPHEN STEINHAUS

Baths With Katie

I still have that picture
The one we always laugh about.
The two of us - 3 years old,
Wet and naked and happy,
Smiling up out of the yellow tub.
Bath crayon reds and blues
Smeared across our tiny tummies,
Rainbow bubbles dripping
From our nearly identical blonde curls.

Those curls are gone now.
Me, I just shave mine off
They haven't been blonde since age eight anyway.
But you, you dyed yours red -
Straightened them, tortured them,
Seared them out with an iron.

And that's how I see you now
Every time I meet you for a drink
So you can introduce me
To another one of your new men -
Be it another malnourished guitar hero
Or some bog-standard, shiftless guy
Who deals out of the kitchen
Of the restaurant where you waitress.
It doesn't really matter,
They all have the same look
A cigarette and unshaven smirk
Until I crush their hand hello.

But you just laugh your laugh -
A hoarse personification
Of Marlboro Lights and Jack and Cokes -
Then you jab a half-drunken red polish finger
Into my chest and say to your newest loser:
Manuel (or Tommy, or whoever it is this week)
This is my oldest friend...
Break my heart, and he kills you.

He laughs until he sees my eyes,
Although I know you would never let me.
It's only when you get up and slide next to me,
Bite my ear lobe or drink my beer
That I see his uneasiness, his jealousy
As you tickle my neck and purr:
We used to bathe together.

It's usually then that he gets up
To make a call, get a drink, get away.
And I always want to follow him
Touch the shoulder of your black leather he wears
And tell him to relax, take it easy
But I don't, and neither does he.

KELLY PILGRIM

The Watcher

On dark blue sheets
you are spread out like a starfish

You never notice me slide sideways
pouring my body out of bed

and I am pleased

because if you woke
what would happen to these
moments of quiet

my early morning silent films
where you're the star?

KELLY PILGRIM

Toulouse-Lautrec is Dead

Toulouse-Lautrec took a lethal dose.
The critic said he was a guy with a hell of a nerve
and a lot of guts; his drawings and colours didn't beat around the bush.
Big simple patches of white and black and red, that was his scam.

The critic said he was a guy with a hell of a nerve.
Nobody could match him at snagging the snouts of capitalist pigs.
Big simple patches of white and black and red, that was his scam.
Chowing down with loose chicks who licked them on the snout.

Nobody could match him at snagging the snouts of capitalist pigs.
At night they snuck out and peeled the posters off walls,
Chowing down with loose chicks who licked them on the snout.
The poster boy put fizz into the lives of bohemian types.

At night they snuck out and peeled the posters off walls;
the flaunting of female bodies, the alcoholic haze.
The poster boy put fizz into the lives of bohemian types,
the promise of a world removed from all routine.

The flaunting of female bodies, the alcoholic haze,
he was as sad as the faces he painted.
The promise of a world removed from all routine.
Out of any calm he cultured chaotic freedom.

He was as sad as the faces he painted,
his drawings and colours didn't beat around the bush.
Out of any calm he cultured chaotic freedom,
sipping the cocktail of art and fantasy from a rusted cup.

BRON BATEMAN

On Seventeen
for Mark

We measure our years
in cups of tea
and soft, familiar kisses.
I cannot inscribe
your secret places with
Here Be Dragons,
for long ago
I mapped the coast
of your body.

I have danced
my fingers
in those parts
reserved for lovers;
planted my flag and
staked my claim
to your flesh.

Yet
 - and here's the joy -

near sleep and falling
towards you
like water,
memory is sluiced clean.
Your dear face
seems new;
as if I had closed my eyes
and slept all winter.

BRON BATEMAN

the promise of rest

I cleared the china cabinet,
with its Sunday-school-straight back,
made music with my fingers
on the nesting cups. I held each piece

toward the light; my hand a ghost
through the saucers' skin;
then filled the cup I'd chosen
with Twining's tea, and milk.

*

And when it one day slipped
between my fingers,
a kaleidoscope of coloured
bones lay splintered at my feet.

I carefully wrapped each piece
in tissue, soft as though
it were a frightened bird
whose song I'd grown to love.

ANDREW DETHERIDGE

2084 A.D.
(for Miroslav Holub)

In this year (which, of course, no longer exists)
Big Brother banned all numbers over 2.
That way, nobody could plan a revolution
as they'd never know their own strength in numbers.
Everyone began working all day and all night
as it never got round to 5 o'clock.
Quotas were always reached,
as they were never more than 2
(though nobody knew by what extent they had been exceeded -
just that it had been more than twice as much).
People couldn't get angry any more - because they could
no longer count to 10 to calm themselves down again.
Gambling became infeasibly easy,
so everyone began to feel noticeably more contented,
thinking themselves to be permanently
on a lucky streak (though, of course, the jackpot
was never more than twice the stake).

In fact, the whole transition went remarkably smoothly,
the whole process being expertly organised
by sound engineers across the nation who,
of course, were totally unaffected by the changes
and who continued, oblivious, exactly as before:

one two
one two
one two

JOHN McPARTLIN

Counting the days

Always the head gardener before us casuals.

Supposing it was his, he dressed the part:
his tie-pin dimpling down his collar-wings;
his hunter's fob-chain hammocked when he stooped;
his warhead boots buffed every day.

Hunter-gatherer. Swaying on sumo feet,
baboon arms low, he straddled strawberry beds.
When springback traps clamped moles,
excitement spittled on his pipe-stem.
When pigeon beaks sheared young sprouts
to crude topiary, he pelleted revenge.

One mudslip day of flooding petulance,
he failed to trench the celery for blanching.
And then, one blue hot day, he swayed
when hoeing bamboo slender artichokes.

As if now there were no pleasing weathers.

At my going, his grumbled sesame
(*Hope ye get oan at the College. Ah think ye will*)
scarcely delayed his plum-gathering.
He waved a drunken wasp within a fruit,
a fist against elaborate farewells.

Now bountiful with cars, tarred h-block bays
draw coldframe blinds over where he worked.

And pose some problem page arithmetic
concerning given moletrap sums of days.

JOHN McPARTLIN

Dyed in the wool

One day he club-coloured green his crinkled hair
which antlered to endive.

The scathing mirror, cracked and pitted,
colandered his confidence,
reduced him to hyperbole.

Succour to the cause,
he had always bought the strip,
the jersey never knowingly undersold,
watched it dance behind the glass door,
enzyme frenzied in biological performance,
following the dosing ball.

Then to be dried out, ironed out.
Like a reformed man. Across the board.

Its foundation dated heart badged its promise.

Its dayglo hoops warned against the Black Gapsite.
As paramedics would, or roadmen, or Fire and Rescue.
All responsible.

A Gapsite so deeply welcoming
as that below the cliff edge
the silent, stoic impi overmarched
on the orders of the Chief
to demonstrate their discipline.

Whereas he would put himself out
to snort and posture
at where he drew the line
between himself and Other.

In static kickdance choreography.

Until, that is, that endive hair day
when (almost heart-stopping that was),
he recognised himself as Other.

But so momentarily,
flailed in the mirror's coloureds short programme,
he could then admire himself again,
a kaleidoscope of monochrome.

And so with confidence resume.

JOHN ROBINSON

Lying Drunk and Naked

We're lying drunk and naked
on these two pushed-together holiday beds.
Jacqueline strokes my face
and gets interested in the laughter lines around my eyes.
She stretches the skin across my cheekbone.
Be careful, I say,
You're letting all my history fall out of there.
Jack likes this idea and gets up on her elbows
to watch bits of fluff, old passport photos
bus tickets, discarded lines from flawed poems
wage slips, fragments of the programme
from the 1966 World Cup Final
tumble down my cheek.
She talks about the loving times
the sorrowful times
the cheese sandwich and cocoa times
and tells me this could be lost
to the knife of the plastic surgeon I've never dreamt
of consulting.
Then she falls asleep
so we don't make love until the morning.

It's nice to do it
in the broad, plain, sober sunshine
with the days stretching far ahead
and all your history
hanging
out.

LEANNE BUNCE

at the gay bar

i can't
sit here
longer
and not mention
this club
is full
of midgets
i said

it's snow white
sharon answered
at the palladium -
dwarves
and understudies
out on the town

we looked
at the one in leather
punching the beat
fists clenched

GERALDINE ROBERTS

Huer's Hut

We huddled under the Huer's hut,
All gregarious giggles under a grey sky
My bridesmaids and I.
Always good for a laugh us
Good time girls,
We survivors of the storm
Who've kept so many warm
That weren't worth the fire.

I'll marry in pink I think
For white is nothing to me,
Virago, Banshee.
We'll have the time of our lives
Working through St. Ives
Burying our faces in fishermen's jumpers
Burying our principles under fishermen's boats.

We play where we can,
Paying the piper, not calling the tune.
For shores are sometimes sad like fairgrounds.

I watch the children, the starfish, the buckets and spades,
And the wind whips my face as my eyes fill with salt.

In the Cornish fishing industry the huer's job was to watch for shoals of
pilchards and alert the fishermen. Today, Cornwall is still full of huers' huts.

BARBARA DANIELS

Turning Point

Just watch their lips as he begins to speak,
(the wine is poured, the table neatly set
for two). It's Friday and the working week
must be deleted, shredded. They'll forget
its horrors as they drizzle vinaigrette.
He deals in futures - somewhat mandarin?
Oh, no! His hands get dirty and his grin
is bloodied, sweating. All her tomorrows
are safe with him. Another glass? He'll win
a thousand battles. Pass the pimentos!

She's at the cutting edge: our heroine
draws for the cat-walk, sleeves up and elbows
sharpened, she'll slash and pinch through thick and thin.
She shows her teeth, seeds her designs and sows
her patterns in a million bungalows.
They'll squeeze the weekend, too, till its pips squeak
in dockland flats, bars, salsa clubs, boutiques.
Time to chill out, he lights a cigarette:
D'you mind? She pouts and turns the other cheek -
she won't fight him, not here, not now - not yet.

GORDON SIMMS

Picking Over Apples

I hear the sigh of tired men sour
as this north-easterly brings dry
flurries to the crocuses,
whipping the high eaves raw.

The last of last year's apples,
Pearmain, Peasegood, Pippin, spaced
on yellow paper, brittle
at the edges: still-life bystanders,
puffing the blossom from their cheeks.

Those worth taking preserve themselves
in bitterness, briny and sharp. The boy
will throw out the others, sickly
with wind-fall, their bruised secret kept
in this silent box-room. Sores and maggots

won't bother him, nor will he screw
his neck to scan old scars of war or earthquake,
flood or famine. He'll fill his bucket

and bounce in free fall, two at a time,
as if it were October - a twist through
the branches, a sashay down the ladder -
supreme, sublime, in bloom, without blemish.

GORDON SIMMS

In the Walled Garden
a reflection on the many chapels of Islay

So many stones eroded, granules of bitten grit
sheered off. The wind takes care of everything,
furnishing the moss with sharp sand, smothering
indecipherable legends in the grass. Here lieth,
there lieth...we guess, painful and slow,
doing our best to estimate the rest in a shadow-play
of hands, a breadth of anonymity scoured from the west.

Grains sweep in from Kilchiaran, Kilchoman
and Kilnenain, from the nameless cilla
of forgotten saints slung along the cedilla
of the Rhinns: gathering in the lap of Islay
between Gruinart and the beaches of Indaal.
Faith grows in this cradle, buffeted by superstition,
staked to the call of exile that would choke the land.

Here the gale is parried with simple deflections,
the collection of particles, painful and slow -
a putting down of roots, a kind of pioneering,
turning the past like a spit of peat,
working hidden names into a fertile tilth.
Let the dead build their walls to honour the living.
May the living rejoice that the dead take care of themselves.

JULIA WIXLER

Something like home

In this endless estate of Braille crescents
blind windows stare vacantly towards Sunday,
waiting for the anonymous hammering
to tap-tap an extra eye for a Cyclops bungalow
or a brief cut of music to dash across the valley
and complete itself in memory.

It isn't home; its symmetry is unfamiliar,
its code unbroken - doors closed and curtained against
a spy ring of mirrors mounted on lounge walls.
Boundaries shuffle tighter and tighter, until
territory is smaller than the length of the garden,
the distance to the front gate.

Only on hot days when the soles of your bare feet
learn the heat of variously coloured slabs,
scuff the grip of non-slip ripples on steep slopes
down to the shops; only then when the shape
of the grit imprints itself in your skin do you feel
something like home entering in.

JULIA WIXLER

Vacant Possession

These rooms are empty
but for the last few boxes,
the mouldy curtains
(sold on for thirty pounds),
and long hairs left knotted
in corners the Hoover
couldn't reach.

We have sold a dream
soiled by the constant
rub of habits: blackened
finger nails and dirty jeans,
wine stains, loose change
dropped inside the sofa - some things
are never reclaimed.

Each breath, each foot-
fall fits inside another
behind the yellow nets
that hang in shame for our neglect.
And as there's nothing left to say,
at 2 p.m. the phone-line ends
in silence.

At three, the electricity
starved of coins - fizzes to its death.
And seven years shut down to sleep
inside a tomb that next week
will enclose the newly-weds
and their first few boxes
stacked in empty rooms.

THACHOM POYIL RAJEEVAN

Anatomy

the head
an aerodrome always kept open
for any aircraft to land

the eyes
two spy satellites
sleepless among the clouds

the limbs
desert paths
leading nowhere

the heart
a harbour
that has faded from the maps

the word
a prison
more ancient than history

in the swamps of flesh
banks, hospitals, hotels
slums where riots break
night after night
dream's broadcast stations
silent and still
the smoke
of unconditional burnout

in the dark
in the blood and semen-stained
crematorium
the thandava of
an underworld city.

THACHOM POYIL RAJEEVAN

He who was gone thus

in the archaeological museum
during an interlude when there were no visitors

the yet-to-be-identified human statue
returned to its past

from a corridor of dead clocks
a door opened
to times hidden
in the dark alleys
the lampposts of exhausted light
bloomed once again

from the memories of the soil
resurrected cities
the ships anchored in water-oblivion
set sailing.

those missing
reappeared as paths on land
and canals in the sea

from both sides of the road
the vanquished,
before the waves drowned them
and the abandoned, were crying:
only this far to go
only this far...

beyond dark years
the dawn-less forests grew dense
the paths that end abruptly

far away, in the valley
or nearby, on the mountaintop
the feeble voice of the guide,

the surprise curves
where the lone tusker, tusks broken, wounded
lies in wait,
the loved ones imagined into being from the opposite side
the prakrit of streams
the arrow-struck songs
of koels
dead before having seen a spring
the solitary gestures of trees
blossoming flowers and birds
the primeval silence of the rocks
pregnant with statues and springs

the ones hunted in their own caves
are being uprooted,
leaving behind weapons and languages,
roots severed and branches withered;
until the forest inside impregnated with seasons
burns down to ashes outside.

the sand-whirls where camels die writhing
the oases like touch of love at height of fever
the fire-winds that rise out of blue
the clouds that fade without raining
like dreams
in the depths of fire-moments
the sea-pyres burned.

the ones who, on their own wounds, journey
return after the diabolic years of failed voyages
flesh rotten, shedding scales
and lay down ready for self immolation
on shores where screams do not echo
till the tranquil white sky above
turned a tumultuous red.

all the visitors have left
the lamps have gone out one by one
the gods, emperors
prophets and poets

all have vanished
in the dark
when orphaned once again
the female statuette - body broken in a battle or an earthquake -
queries a be-headed male statue:

in which way
and which state of nirvana
oh Lord,
this posture
as stone and mud.

GEOFF STEVENS

A day at the office

Burroughs loaded again,
and soon the canvas blasted into holes.
He surveys his art work,
standing there in pinstripe, button-down shirt
and brown fedora,
his parchment skin decomposing
under the crisp, clean clothing.
He sees an image to aim for
and exploits it with a close-up blast of shot.
He knows that someone on this silly planet
will pay big bucks for it.
He ponders on it,
thoughts echoing around his New York bunker.
He rolls them around at dinner
and swallows them down with a Jack Daniels.
He will spew them out later,
words cut up and pasted,
all over the ancient typewriter.
The man is some chancer.

BRIAN CONNELL

Another Recipe For A Bedsit

Take one landlord and hit with baseball bat.
Insert knife into throat of landlord
and cut open.
Ignore screams or if screams bother you
insert large plug into mouth of landlord.
Begin to chop up landlord's body,
the shaking of the limbs
the sobbing
and the bloody nerve splintering screaming
will soon subside
as landlord dies.
Roast landlord on spit
and invite friends round.
Maybe keep a landlord arm
or leg for leftovers.

Landlords will freeze well
if kept
in the same condition
as tenants.

TERRY STOTHARD

Valentine's Day 1995
(i.m. of a father born on 14 February 1909 who died in April 1976)

Most of the birds have deserted the cemetery,
they have no wish to be scavenging today
something more important is on their minds...

...it isn't how he expected it.
No zombies, no widows wailing,
no suspect stranger lingering.
The duffel-coated boy sidesteps
a knot of vivid wreaths.

A few headstones have shifted;
lean like cards in a drunkard's hands.
Bushes and shrubs are bursting free
though strands of frost ensnare
their roots in a cobweb.

Three women shuffle, suffuse into
each other for droplets of solace;
only the new-mown grass smells
of anything like hope.

The boy stoops to steal a single rose
from a brimming grave, replaces it.
He no longer believes in a God
but lacks the faith of a true atheist.

He breaks a daffodil from a bed
leaves it marooned on the freshest mound,
the solitary star
in a muddy night sky.

Standing up he wipes his nose
on his sleeve, walks away.
He never went to the funeral
doesn't know if it's the right grave,
felt it was something he had to do...

...that is what should have happened.
Instead he's nineteen years too late.
He's not sure if he's forgiven but he knows
today is about finding love from the hate
he scavenged from sudden shocking loss.

TERRY STOTHARD

Blitzed

The flat, like his mind, is infested with midges.
Tiny clones, indestructible as 'roaches;
kill one and two inherit its space.
Noisome aerosol spray diffuses with stale air
but the midges have minute gas masks;
hardly notice the chemical mist.

Candy floss strands of cobwebs hang,
wiry branches swollen with overripe fruit.
Spiders scuttle chaotically from trap to trap,
like late buses between stops,
the unexpected banquet too much:
frantic, angry, ready for their winter holiday.

Newspapers, dead as yesterday's hope,
lie unopened, slightly curled at their edges,
stained with insects flat as full stops.
Ill-fitting windows, murky with gatecrashers,
are shut to keep the uninvited away.
The red carpet has stirring puddles of black life.

Exhausted by the relentless strafing
his mongrel wags a half-hearted welcome,
he's acceded to the throng,
hopes that soon he, too, will have his day.
He makes an occasional snap at the hoards,
then hawks black clumps from his tongue.

In the static rocking chair a man nestles
a coffee, its meniscus dark with kamikaze
six-legged pilots. He nods his head
to my greeting, like a boss to a worker.
I ask, *Is this what the blitz was like?*
No, he slurs, *I knew I'd survive the blitz.*

TERRY STOTHARD

Like a Librarian

It's his silences that worry her
the not knowing if he's sulking.
She prefers the blood-red flashes
of angry eyes to the passive whites
of indifference, the surrendering flag
of his hand, the begrudging *Oh, alright*.
These moods of his make her feel

like a spinster librarian who takes pity
on the hobo sheltering from rain,
who can't bring herself to stare
at the vagabond or scrutinise herself
naked in the full length mirror;
who can't bear the sight of flesh
watermarked by years of hiding in books

who feels only distaste at deep driven
nooks that should have seen
more of light bulbs and daylight;
felt the more urgent palms
of every male whose eye
she had caught instead of
turning the page on a novel.

Doesn't he know how she shivers
when his fingers brush her skin
and his innocent eyes look up,
seemingly too sensitive for sin,
until she cries, *Enough!*
and lets him have it his way
but only for a one-night loan.

TERRY STOTHARD

Rules of the game

The doorway is dark,
clad in Yorkshire stone that's raggedy
as coats on death-shop rails.
Night has imbibed its twilight draught,
the street lamp has ripened
from embryo orange to adult gold.

The street has its own black life:
murmuring cats, snuffling stray dogs.
Her heels' clear echoes are slurred
by cobbles as she nears her pitch;
solemn-faced, no happy-go-lucky
blue movie hooker fantasy.

Sporting lurid glitz
(first rule: glamour attracts)
she remains in the shadows,
scans the street for police,
loosens blouse buttons,
inspects laddered fishnets.

She leans against the doorway jamb
forms an impure hypotenuse.
Her eyes flash sexual conspiracy
in rehearsed routine. Her show stops
to smile at a friend. Her rouged lips
pout enticement at a merry stag.

He zigzags away, a fish off the hook,
amid a murky stream of alibis.
Her thickened lashes flutter contempt
diffused with self-pity;
(second rule: drunks don't haggle)
she sees me and her cabaret returns.

She offers me everything but she's
offering me nothing. Part of me says Yes.
Yes to the girl too quick for childhood
but too slow for her own good.
I don't say yes, I don't want to drag her down,

not to where I am.

The next doorway is dark.

KATY DARBY

Participant Observation

1. This the black whole of his heart
  when I reached my hand in as though
  into a gutted tree's uncertain depth, and grasped
  not solid walls, but nothing. A scribbled cave
  so wide and empty, echoes could not span it,
  like the space between electrons.

a) After twenty years of theory he'd deduced I must exist,
  explaining matter out of darkness, and dividing the percentage
  of my likelihood by zero. All his safety lay in numbers.
  And I geigered our decay while he was busy counting miracles
  and anniversaries of days, and angels, pinned like markers
  to each charmed quark of happiness.

b) *Cats in impossible boxes*, was his judgement of us, later.
  I agreed, not quite recalling if it mattered; or if so, why
  he was grasping still for proofs too marvellous to be conjecture
  as the vacuum in his intercostal spaces filled with fallout.
  Love's a thought experiment, I told his silence, being witty;
  but he didn't laugh, just stared, unanswerable as a lab-rat.

2. And if I boil it all back down to science, to
  machinery of glance on glance, or the tooled
  fit of flesh to bone, I find I am, as he is still, alone.
  So my evangelistic pessimism tells me
  nothing can be proved or certain, and that
  merely by observing we can change the thing observed.
  And all the truths we held to be self-evident
  and beautiful, the equal and the opposite
  of loving/being loved, such elegant hypotheses
  exist to be disproved.

KATY DARBY

Case-worker

His battered suitcase of a heart,
he touted it with him everywhere:
flogging his trinkets to the flotsam,
the passing-through, gape-mouthed
sly-eyed. Who'll buy
the happiness that can't be found
in bottles with plagiaristic names?
Ladies
and gentlemen, discards lonely
in night-time stations, in cunning alleys -
This Rolex is love. Look at the workmanship!
Listen - bend closer - o listen to that
sweet tick! Each stroke is a promise
madam, a vow that must be kept,
treasured, like the friable
machinery of joy. I sell you nothing
if not dreams in beautiful boxes. Come buy!

Here's the rub. Hawking behind
his split and polished suitcase stall
he sells his wares at a loss. Each Oyster
nestled in its plastic case, contains a pearl;
each perfume bottle has upon
its peeling label, poetry of love
the secrets of the heart in five
languages. He swears -
each beat of the pulse, each tick
a sacred vow - it's
the genuine article. Accept no subterfuge.

In the striplit cities, millstoned by
the weight of gold at his chest, dazzled
by the scent of passion and immortality
whispering through the cracks, the locks
burst on his battered suitcase of a heart
jewelling the tarmac with rubies, and the tick

holds its breath as long as a promise,
a broken bargain
unnoticed by the midnight traffic, passing.

CAROLYN GARWES

Beachcombers

The child and her grandmother comb the beach,
searching for pretty shells or interesting driftwood.
She knows that shells are houses and cajoles
the older woman into tales of absent owners.

She draws a street on the damp sand and places
her finds along it in a row. *This one's out to lunch*,
the storyteller starts. *Like Grampa*, her listener
interjects. Bright child, she's heard people talking.

On their return home, she rushes right away
to show her grandfather all her marbled pebbles,
her bright bits of smoothly sanded glass
and other jetsam. His little salvage queen.

She fetches more of her seashore bounty.
Climbing on his lap, she turns him into Neptune,
with straggly strands of seaweed hair
and a crown of shells and seagull feathers.

Siren sweet, she tries to charm him with her shanties.
Tied to his chair, his ears are stopped.
He doesn't hear her. If he even knows she's there,
there's no outward recognition.

This is a **fallen** king - washed-up, empty,
stranded high above the watermark.
His little mermaid croons the treasures of her day
into the conches of his ears. There's no one home.

GERALD WATTS

A Man in His Prime

Between the years of over-manly handshakes
And the trouble that was yet to come,
There was a summer afternoon when
He lounged in a garden chair and threw
Tennis balls for my infant daughter
To collect.

He'd already begun to shrink, of course,
As they do, around the neck and the hips.
But the stocky build, the gimlet eye,
The handsome face - a lot of Spencer Tracey,
A hint of Mr Punch - were much
As they had always been.

Mussing her hair, laughing as she nearly
Tripped, (*What a pretty girl!*), he suddenly
Tilted back his head and began to sing -
A hymn, a psalm, a chorus from the opera
All in such an unexpected voice: warm and sweet,
Young and resonant.

In quick succession he became: a chorister,
A crooner, a performer on the stage. I listened, charmed
And privileged. Then, after some lines of Vera Lynn,
He winked at me and said: *Of course, the Germans*
Had the best tunes and, when no one was around,
That's what we'd sing.

With tapping foot, he sang *im Deutsch* a Wermacht
Drinking song and followed that with *My Lili Marlene.*
I glimpsed him fully then, in his prime, in his naval cap,
Singing under his breath, as he eased his torpedo boat
Along the coast of Sicily, the war-weary clouds
Lit by a conspiratorial moon.

GERALD WATTS

This Evening I See How

This evening I see how
The smelting sun uses
The clouds and the cliffs
To mould a pig-iron sea.

And I watch the way
The wind sends out sudden,
Quick-footed shadows
To turn the wheat to water.

I notice, too, that
The sky is a marble dome
And that small stones run
Crab-wise under my heels.

Ahead of me the fencepost crows
Sing like choristers: *Have faith,*
They sing, *Have faith in the sun*
And the wind and the watery wheat.

Commend yourself to them.
So I stop and I turn
And I let myself fall
Backwards, arms outstretched.

Backwards, arms outstretched
Falling onto the restless, waiting wheat
Which rolls its countless heads
Beneath my back and bears my weight.

And so, gently jostled and tickled
By the flowing, whiskered wheat,
I am borne, belly up, toes skyward,
Away from the path and the pig-iron sea
Towards the sun and the far horizon.

PAT WATSON

Relative Values

They came in glorious technicolour:
Auntie Vi, in purple velvet,
brigadier's moustache and bass profundo voice
- a man in drag? -
along with Auntie May, in scarlet slacks,
(what would the neighbours say?)
and, false as teeth, Aunt Millie, all dolled up
in powder blue, to match her roving eyes.
Then came the men: Our Ron,
in shiny serge from Moss Bros, doling out
the bags of sweets and slabs
of toffee from the Bull Ring,
Uncle Vern, a bookie's runner in a shabby mac,
as shifty as a ferret, all on edge
from dodging coppers.

Drinking pots of tea they sat around
the kitchen table, trying to ignore
my mother looking daggers by the fire -
the visitors were none of her concern,
come down as she had since she married him -
while he, jammed in a corner, sheepishly
enjoyed their banter and their Brummie wit,
teasing each other over long-past larks, until
Tata a bit! and in a sudden flurry
they were gone to catch the bus,
taking with them their noise
and all their colour, leaving us alone
in black and white again, and very,
                                    very
                                        quiet.

RICHARD PALMER

Turning into father

My face shaven in the mirror.
Lines bisect around the eyes and chin
Cutting through memory towards another face .

Frustrated eyes caught in the driver's mirror
Pierce back. The G reg Honda
Reverses to an old blue Volkswagen.
Part of me shrinks to the passenger seat
While the rest curses traffic.

I have tried to emulate those legs
That once played football, hockey and cricket
Though the pain caught me in the back of the thigh:
The string of muscle drawn suddenly tight
As a butcher's parcel.

I remember your impatience
As I failed to add the figures in my head
Your eyes slicing down the columns
While the edges drifted away from my focus.

These days your eyes blur before a map.
I point out the way to go
And you ask me the name again.

Like you, my vacillations are policed
By the sound of my mother's voice
Having to do it all herself.

Each time I forget is a nail
Knocked into the future.
I long to bring you columns to add up
But it is all done by calculator now.

We grow together.
My face, so like my mother's
It was remarked on in shops,
Takes on your features.

You are older, but I will catch up.

MARK BORG

Last Suppers
for my friend, Veronica

She is numb to every word,
every gesture of her friends,
no matter how touching.

She no longer cares in any immediate sense.
What she used to feel
is now just a distant nag of memory.

The withering of her body
is too literal for family and friends,
who become figurative in her presence,

skirting the tricky subject of their good health
as if they did her a favour.
They forget their saturation in life,

take for granted the dripping of their vitality
around her house, the scattered shoes and draped coats.
There are long silences within and without herself.

People forget to call,
or ring off before
her crooked hand can thud the button.

Neighbours come, then go almost before they've been,
leaving milk and bread, their absences lingering
in the warm scent of suppers seeping from foil.

ERIC SMITH

Slow march

Silence, moved by softened pads
of muted drums and brass,
before the slow thunder moves to a kind of tune,
whose movement is essentially rhythm.
So much of the step is the noiseless
glide of the balletic tip to the precise
point below where the tip must land.
The full fall follows.

The public gently sways
as the throbbing deepens, the march
goes ever onward to its own eternity.
The boots are polished every day
like the tools of a craftsman.

And such it is, a ritual beyond its end
and in itself a piece of art
to be laboriously raised once
and again from a dead piece of paper.
Its hope is on the very edge of time,
channelling through the watering eyes
to some legacy now unknown,
vibrant through the body
(young men, you may cry)
to the fastidiousness of those feet.

TAMSIN FORMAN

Party Frock

Pinned to a grass stem
A gossamer skin
Sloughed from a viper
Lifts up on the air.

Sequined with rain drops
Glass-bugled with dew,
Exquisite, zig-zagged
Haute snaky *Couture*.

Pale as a moonstone,
A silk chiffon shift
Shrugged off when the dawn
Broke, After the Ball.

DIANA SYDER

Snow, Eyam Edge

Clouds pour out of heaven
onto Longstone Edge,
hilltop and heavy air rolled into one.
A blast of white and the ground
has dropped away to all
these blank, astounding distances.

To the south, the world ends
in a doom of smoke and snow
pillowing behind Chesterfield.

Northward, the lemon silver light
is a great lake lapping the rim of the parted clouds,
a sky giftwrapped and opened up
into something unfrozen, beyond,
to be walked into or turned
towards with a vaulting heart.

It doesn't come plainer
than this epic of dark and light.
Up here, nothing hides or is hidden,
my span is endless,
the balance right,

as the eye of the universe
turns tender for a moment
above the creaking cradle of earth.

SIMON PICKERING

Elle

That magazine you buy for company
each time we travel,
kept us quiet
until, at length, the food arrived
and you tired of shopping tips and
models wearing fancy dress.
But while you slept
I read on, through *One Hundred Ways*
To Please Your Man
and why he must
forget his mum, *and learn*
to accept you as you are,
and the bra which makes your tea;
until the Duty Free appeared
and you woke up,
all thought of terror gone
as the steward bagged your
Calvin Klein and two hundred
cigarettes.

JUAN CARLOS VARGAS

Circus

Oasis in air, a clown atop a spreading
Stain of blue light, footboard and frame

Tethered to gondolas of flight recede
Before the teeterboard's touch, tossed

Orbits upshot to sutured canopy then all
Dims to blue light in this tent's tottering

Moons of height and still patches of loops
Shower us in gentle applause swaying

Here below. The fife and drum, a twirl of hands,
Sleights-of-hand spawn crazed signatures of birds,

Affirm the depths of air like seeds unvined
And regiments of clowns collide and juggle

Pennants, ringmaster, nets to the ground.
A birling pole off-balance, a hatted quilt

Of candles hail scaffolds of chairs buoyed now
Neither by rope nor wood but jagged nooning

Light, a palace in the rough of green sunned by
Drawbridges to the child's delight who chides us

For that we fail to cherish most, these moments
Of lost and found, and teaches us finally that this

Is better than that, or any triangular jigsaw
Or sporting freefalls the world, or we, applaud.

KATHY DAVIES

Owls

You said: *A pair of owls live in this wood*
and then you added, *Keep me company.*
I did not know whether you meant the owls
or if you were inviting me to stay -
your head was turned away, the emphasis
was lost. I did not give you a reply.
You said: *One will come now. It is the time.*

We waited. In the stillness tiny sounds
came near: a bee, the distant bleats of sheep
some laughing boys outside the village pub.
A motorbike tore through the green evening
behind us. After that came true silence.
We screwed up our eyes against the sunset.
House-martins flickered in the last, high light.

Our thoughts flew far away from each other.
Then, without us knowing, the owl was there
so close on the branch of the wild cherry.
That is its post, you said, as though the owl
were a sentry and the wood a castle.
It swivelled round its saucer-face and stared,
its feathers reddening in the low sun's rays.

She may well be a female owl, I said.
She has a queenly air. Her consort called
and in her soft, low voice she answered him.
And when the darkness came she launched herself
into the night, seeing all before her
clearly as if it were the day. I thought
this could be any time in history.
The owls have not changed. I pictured, under
leaves, the jewel-eyed mice blind to their fate.

I fumbled for your hand, seeing and not seeing,
knowing and not knowing that you wanted me to stay.

KATHY DAVIES

Removals

I go back each day,
slowly subtracting the last of my things
from the wrong sum of our life together:
the hoya, still half-crying its nectar tears;
the lopsided pottery bowl I made;
my wooden writing box, empty inside.
The key turns familiarly in the lock;
it is a shock to think that this is not my home.
On the mat our letters lie together awkwardly.

I wander through the rooms.
They're still the same but with just your things now.
The wardrobe gapes at its loss.
Touching your pillow, the smell of your hair,
almost makes me cry, sitting there,
on the edge of the bed you've hardly slept in until now.
But I know, as I pick up your socks,
we never made a pair.

My hips come to rest against the kitchen sink.
The daytime street is quiet,
a gap left where you parked last night.
But you won't look up and wave when you come home
and I won't smile.

On my trips to the car,
a neighbour glances up between his flashing shears
suspiciously, as though I am a thief.
The air is heavy with lavender and unfallen rain.
Tomorrow I will have no reason to be here.

JILL ELLIS

Potato Peeler

In some far distant time
digging down the levels,
reaching for history,
a hand more wise than mine
may close round this -

an artefact no artisan would own.

A turn of wood
bound to a turncoat blade.
Unfinished - pointless
with snag-edged slits
like conjunctival eyes.

It has the look of drudgery,
the weight of blighted dreams,
the feel of dreary domesticity.

This was no ritual object
seasoned with romance.

It never flashed
from an assassin's hand
to ride the night
and bed its blade
in flesh

or found itself
apprentice to a sorcerer
and on some marble altar
inscribed the entrails
to inform his necromantic art.

Lost forever to my hand
its ending then will echo mine.

Examined and identified,
the records filled and filed.
Then will come the rite of cleansing,
the linen cloths.
Finally, when all is done,
laid in a box.

Forgotten.

JANE RUSBRIDGE

Travelling Rug
for David

My mother squandered hers
on tar-pebbled English beaches,
tenting us against the anorak wind.

My auntie's, four-folded flat
in the boot of her annually colour-changed mini,
might be spread under picnic blue skies.

We found ours in Brittany
one Cinderella summer when
we couldn't have paid
for a souvenir, or the mussels

you collected daily;
fabrique en France, like the garlic
on our wined fingers and breath.

Sand-heavy and solid with salt,
it was hunched stiffly beside
the black-feathered barbecue stumps.

Wary, we waited all day
before we claimed its warmth
and brought it home.

JANE RUSBRIDGE

The Cockle Shell

That last summer in France,
I collected shells in your old straw hat.
Damp sand slid
through the golden lattice, between my fingers,
from the slack empty jaws.

You told me that live cockles,
between the hinged, heart-shaped shells,
have a foot, muscular, pointed,
and used for locomotion. I remember your hands
cupped, as you told me about the mantle,

the two lobes of tissue
that secrete the shell in layers, a chitinous outer
layer, a middle layer
or aragonite, and a laminated inner layer. The empty
shells are used for buttons.

Poised on its porcupine curve
beside brittle, bright china, the largest
cockle fanned its precise
hostility daily on our blue kitchen shelf,
in shades of sand and skull.

Talon-gouged grooves
raise ridges thick and spiked, like
fathomless medieval weaponry
held in my hand, and protecting,
in the smooth, tooth-shiny chamber,

nothing now.

THE POETS

JOCELYN SIMMS: "I wrote my first poem in 1996 when my children fled the nest. My poetry tends to be personal and I am delighted that *Mischanter* has been awarded a prize. I co-founded The Writers' Block with my husband, Gordon, in 1999. The emphasis is on beating the censor and encouraging the flow of creativity. We have published an anthology of the group's work, *The Usual Suspects.*"

MARGARET EDDERSHAW: worked for 25 years in the UK as an actor, director and university teacher of theatre. She has published on Brecht and Stanislavsky and several of her plays have been performed at the Edinburgh Festival and in London 'fringe' theatres. In 1995 she left Britain to live in Greece and since then she has had over 50 poems published in anthologies and magazines and has given readings in Athens. She has produced two collections: *Riding the Rainbow* (travel poems) and *Second Homing* (poems about Greece), of which the total sale price (£3) for each copy is donated to Oxfam (available via sturgess@naf.forthnet.gr)

STEPHEN STEINHAUS: born and raised in the west of Chicago, Stephen has been an English literature teacher, bouncer and singer in Hawaii, California and England. He, his wife and two sons now permanently reside in Stratford-upon-Avon, where Stephen is a college lecturer in performing arts. He also fronts Set Against, a Coventry hard-core band, and Dr. Teeth's Big Band, a Stratford-based jazz/swing outfit.

BRON BATEMAN: born in Albany, Western Australia in 1964. She is married with seven children. Ragged Raven is publishing a collection of poems by Bron and by Kelly Pilgrim in June 2002. Bron is particularly interested in marginalised bodies and the way in which experience is inscripted on the flesh.

KELLY PILGRIM: born in Perth, Western Australia in 1969. Ragged Raven is publishing a collection of poems by Kelly and by Bron Bateman in June 2002. Her work has been published in literary magazines and journals in Australia. She lives in Perth's southern suburbs with her partner and many animals.

ANDREW DETHERIDGE: born in 1969. He has taught at schools in the West Midlands and is now a lecturer in English and poet in residence at Sandwell College. His poems and haiku have been published in magazines and anthologies worldwide and he has won or been placed in several national poetry competitions.

JOHN McPARTLIN: based sometimes in Edinburgh, sometimes in Clackmannanshire. He recently retired from school teaching to concentrate on poetry writing and has been published by, among others, Ver Poets, Poetry Scotland, Anchor Books and Poetry Now. *Dyed in the wool* presents the obsessive football supporter whose worst moment of weakness is seeing a mirror image of himself so like that of the enemy supporter that his 'raison d'etre' momentarily collapses until he recovers by donning again his colours and armour to regain comfort in self-justification. While the gardener in *Counting the days* is not a social bigot, he is restricted by his self-chosen tasks and preoccupation with them, unaware of the 'cold-frame' which will one day be imposed on him. The poem originates in personal observation of a workaholic obsessive head gardener with whom the poet worked.

JOHN ROBINSON: varied employment - including tripedresser, trucker, journalist. John's first collection of poetry, *the cook's wedding*, was published by Ragged Raven press in 2001. He plays trombone in Hull's no. 1 soul band.

LEANNE BUNCE: "I'm 37 years old and live in Scotland with my partner and foster-dog. I'm studying towards a PhD in Critical and Creative Writing. *At The Gay Bar* is one of two poems to appear in print in March 2002. The other is *Western Charm* being published by The Association of Scottish Literary Studies in their annual anthology, *New Writing Scotland*. I'm a member of the Stirling Writer's Group, and indebted to the group for its literary support and encouragement. I'm also indebted to my partner for continual in-house editing of my writing."

BARBARA DANIELS: started to write poetry late in life and has three collections of poems published by the NPF: *Dance With Me*, *Spin Again* and *Mean Time*. She won the Poetry Monthly Open Poetry Booklet Competition for 2001 with a selection called *Camera Obscura*. Also due for publication are a Pikestaff pamphlet, *Take Off* (autumn 2002), and a Manifold chapbook (2003). Her poetry appears widely in magazines and she is an enthusiastic competition entrant.

GORDON SIMMS: has won 15 poetry competitions since 1997, including the first Ragged Raven, in which he has also been a runner-up. He won an Arvon prize in 1998 and has recently won a one-act play competition. His work has appeared in numerous small press publications and in *The Interpreter's House, Other Poetry, Envoi* and *Connections*. He has read on BBC Radio and at Edinburgh and York Festivals.

JULIA WIXLER: "I was born in Brighton, 1970. I read and write poetry 'just for pleasure' as they say and have done for as long as I can remember. I live in High Wycombe, working as a database specialist for a software company. Occasionally a poem finds its way into a runners-up list or a magazine like *Staple, Pulsar* or *Envoi*.

THACHOM POYIL RAJEEVAN: born and raised in Kerala, the southernmost state in India. Thachom is widely published in India as a poet and essayist writing in English and his mother tongue, Malayalam. A graduate in physics and post-graduate in English language and literature, he began his career as a journalist. He is now working as public relations manager of the University of Calicut, Kerala. In *Anatomy*: thandava is the final cataclysmal dance of the Lord Shiva. In *He who was gone thus*: the title is an inversion of the Buddhist phrase 'thadagata' which means 'Buddha was one who had come thus'; prakrit is one of the ancient languages in India; and nirvana is the final union of the individual spirit with the universal spirit.

GEOFF STEVENS: editor of Purple Patch; co-organiser of Poetry Wednesbury's open mic meetings on the last Wednesday of each month; lives in West Bromwich.

BRIAN CONNELL: lives in Hull, a regular performer of his work.

TERRY STOTHARD: born in Welwyn Garden City in 1962. He started writing poetry again after a long gap about nine years ago. He has had work published in *the new writer, Tabla, Interpreter's House* and several competition anthologies. He has won prizes in the Peterloo Poetry Competition twice and was the winner of last year's Southport Open Poetry Competition. He runs poetry taster workshops for community groups, charities and schools and also works as a basic skills, key skills and creative writing tutor at Waltham Forest College of Further Education.

KATY DARBY: is 25, semi-employed and lives in London. She runs a theatre company and website (www.einekleine.com) and has won prizes for her poetry, short stories and drama. Her poems have appeared in *Stand* magazine and on London buses, and her prose has been published by the *London Magazine*. In *Participant Observation*: part 1, the space between electrons is microscopic, but contains nothing at all - it is the only space in the universe which is truly empty; part a, any number divided by zero becomes infinity; part b, 'cats in impossible boxes' refers to Schrödinger's cat, a thought experiment - the cat in the box may be dead or alive and it is only when you open and observe it that it becomes one or the other; part 2, 'merely by observing we can change the thing observed' - Heisenberg's Uncertainty Principle.

CAROLYN GARWES: is a 'woman returning to poetry' after a gap of thirty years. House, husband and dogs are taking on an air of neglect as she makes up for lost time. She has already had several competition successes and her poems have appeared in small press magazines and anthologies. When she is not celebrating the resurfacing of her Muse, she works as a freelance copy editor and indexer. She lives in a small village in Oxfordshire.

GERALD WATTS: " I am 44 years old and happily married with three children. A history graduate, I was a soldier and a teacher before moving into training and consultancy. I live in Suffolk. *A Man in His Prime* is, I hope, a faithful account of the person - a relation by marriage - and the incident I witnessed. Sadly, he became terminally ill soon after that summer afternoon. *This Evening I See How* was inspired by summer evenings near the coast in the far north east of Scotland; times when nature no longer seems to obey its own rules."

PAT WATSON: has written prose for many years but poetry only recently. Born in Coventry, she wrote *Relative Values* as an affectionate tribute to her father's Birmingham family. She lives in Stratford-upon-Avon.

RICHARD PALMER: "An English teacher for the past 28 years, I live in Berkshire with my wife and baby daughter and I write poems in the interstices of life."

ERIC SMITH: lives in Upton Grey, near Basingstoke. "Nearly 40 years ago I won a first in English at Oxford. I very soon found that teaching at any level was not for me and went to work in a building society. I wrote in my spare time, producing 13 non-fiction books, mainly on clock repairing (which I did as a sideline) and also on pianos and two general books on poetry. I have written poetry for most of my life, won several prizes and contributed to magazines and anthologies."

TAMSIN FORMAN: born Malaya; left ahead of Japanese invasion; brought up in Dorset; lived and worked in Middle East, Africa and Europe; raised family; settled near Oxford, rough out poems in head during daily, hilly walking.

DIANA SYDER: has published two poetry collections, *Hubble* and *Maxwell's Rainbow*, with Smith Doorstop Press. She was awarded a Public Awareness of Science award for her poetry by the Institute of Physics and is poet in residence in the Dept. of Engineering, University of Sheffield, funded by Leverhulme Trust.

SIMON PICKERING: a teacher, lives in Walthamstow, London. *Elle* was written on 21 September 2001 on a FinAir flight to Helsinki.

JUAN CARLOS VARGAS: a U.S. citizen who was born and lives in Costa Rica. His poetry has appeared in journals and magazines, including *The Chicago Review, Voices International, The Caribbean Writer,* and *No Exit.* He teaches American and British literature at the University of Costa Rica and has taught at American universities, including the universities of New Orleans and Rhode Island.

KATHY DAVIES: grew up in a village called Birdingbury and went to school in Warwick; now aged 33 and living in London; doing a part-time M.A. in writing at Middlesex University and writing her first novel while also teaching English part-time at a girls' secondary school.

JILL ELLIS: "I live in Norfolk, near the coast, and work as an adult basic skills tutor. I am secretary of North Norfolk Writers and my other hobbies include walking and natural history, especially birds. As well as poetry, I write short stories, which have a tendency to spookiness if not outright horror. I have had some success with competitions. I think poetry should make the familiar strange. And education, my living, exists to make the strange familiar, so contrary to the opinion of my friends, I consider myself a well balanced human being. I have one daughter who thinks I'm marvellous too!"

JANE RUSBRIDGE: "I grew up by the sea in east Sussex and now live with a farmer just across the road from the sea in west Sussex. The sea seems to be a strong influence on my writing. One of the best decisions of my life was to begin studying for an English degree seven years ago, when my youngest daughter started school. It changed my life in many fundamental ways. I'm now an associate lecturer in English at the same university, and nearing the completion of an MA in creative writing."